T0329062

# Strides of Hope

*Poems*

## Tawanda Chigavazira

Mwanaka Media and Publishing Pvt Ltd,
Chitungwiza Zimbabwe
*
*Creativity, Wisdom and Beauty*

Publisher: *Mmap*
Mwanaka Media and Publishing Pvt Ltd
24 Svosve Road, Zengeza 1
Chitungwiza Zimbabwe
mwanaka@yahoo.com
mwanaka13@gmail.com
https://www.mmapublishing.org
www.africanbookscollective.com/publishers/mwanaka-media-and-publishing
https://facebook.com/MwanakaMediaAndPublishing/

Distributed in and outside N. America by African Books Collective
orders@africanbookscollective.com
www.africanbookscollective.com

ISBN: 978-1-77931-468-0
EAN: 9781779314680

© Tawanda Chigavazira 2023

DISCLAIMER
All views expressed in this publication are those of the author and do
not necessarily reflect the views of *Mmap*.

# Dedication

To

Samuel Chatambudza **Chigavazira,**
My first inspiration, my hero!

(may your soul continue to rest
from the rigors of your toil on earth brother)

# Table of Contents

Acknowledgements
Foreword
Preface

# Acknowledgements

For the inspiration that I drew from your work Edward Dzonze, I thank you very much. Our interaction birthed in me a new zeal to write on until coming up with poems changed from hard-time-mental involvement into a hobby – more like play!
Now, it's a passion.

Special mention also goes to the organisers of LitFest Harare 2018 and the invitation I got from Takudza Chikepe (VaChikepe) which afforded a chance to rub shoulders with literary gurus like Memory Chirere, Chirikure Chirikure and Albert Nyathi. The occasion motivated me on to continue working on my verses.

To my family, without your physical, moral and psychological support, this collection wouldn't have been what it is today. I thank you my wife and kids!

~~**~~

# FOREWORD

The millennium has come to a close, the world shut in a state of deplorability and hopelessness. Wars, poverty, hunger and other phenomenon have ravaged societies and left humanity on the brink of extinction. The world has turned into a bleak entrapping and yet in the eyes of the lone voice, Tawanda Chigavazira, has seen that in the wake of all these debilitating circumstances surrounding human existence, there is always a keg of hope.

In *Strides of Hope*, we are taken into a whole different world where pain is an opportunity to make strides for a higher calling. Circumstances are merely a pedestal towards a higher goal. This is a miscellany like no other, that breathes life into a lifeless society. It evolves around optimism, and the poet is an eye through which we have a glimpse through the chink into the infinite and endless possibilities.

It is a mish-mash of beautiful pieces that are nothing less of a panacea in a world that has become desolate; they are a cry of a lone voice that seeks to trace its path and carve a niche towards transforming a society into a just enclave where tribal and ethnical lines are erased. In *Strides of Hope*, Tawanda Chigavazira is that bold voice that speaks openly of human fears and aspirations in an unbridled way. His words are those war stallions that reflect on human carnal limitations and the glittering flare of hope that lies in persistently pursuing a dream; that great stride, as he opines, starts with a mere step.

From the kiln of poetic excellence, *Strides of Hope* is born. It is that bold declaration of a tried and tested cadre in the field of literary craft and a true companion of all man who seek to understand their purpose in life.

-Professor Ngugi waMkirii-

~~**~~

# Preface

Strides can be short or slow, but they are a sure mode for the attainment of the greater goal of a people's hope! Goals only attained when poetry erases all the tribal lines to create a free people. The words, sentences and verses of the poems in this book are the very *Strides of Hope*. They occupy the gap between our efforts and the accomplishments of our sole desires. The author crafted these poems to provide the kinesis which propels our legs along the long, winding paths to where our hope lies. They are the mental capacitation which stimulates our minds to advocate for a tomorrow that we all wish. In other words, the poems are the catalyst to physical and mental spur towards self-actualisation – towards re-discovery!

'A journey of a thousand miles begins with a single step.' Each poem in this book is a step necessary for the completion of the populace's journey to our *Hopeland*. Without movement, a person is idle or better still deemed dead. 'Idleness brings about want!' The poems herein do not only give legs to 'the people' but ideally enable us to embark on an obvious journey. It is a journey of all night long, until dawn. A walk that will end, only upon the break of dawn! Only when dawn can be seen, sun-raising a sunny day, will the citizenry celebrate these 'strides of hope.'

Strides of hope are the dash to the nearest bolthole by the helpless lot when violence is unleashed at us by men armed to the tooth. They are the hurry-scurry from hopelessness to hopefulness! They are the bold steps towards the propagandist in the morning and spit the poison fed to us the previous day. And before we say goodbye, bravely point out that rainwash was used to do the dishes instead of a dishwasher. Some strides in this collection stumble upon perverts, paedophiles and shame them for a society we all want. A society upholding an unblemished social fabric!

~~**~~

"Be the change
that you wish to see
in the world."

# (Mahatma Gandhi)

# Sexual predators

Almost everywhere, they are always there preying,
Playing tricks on the vulnerability of juvenility,
Paedophiles, sexual predators of the infantile,
Men who unashamedly misuse their masculinity,
Causing the girl child to lose respect of her Father!

Men who prune almost everything on budding roses,
Inhibiting growth of character and sowing fragility,
Like wolfs in sheepskins, they waylay them at blinds
Sprinkling grains of too-good-to-pass baits that bite
The girl-child fall hook, line and sinker to the devilish ploy
They unremorsefully abuse them as if they're entitled to!

Woman of their age shy away from them upon sight.
Because they know some of the dicey games they played!
Woe to them men who prey on the innocence of juveniles.
Senile terrestrial Devils, introspect and earn respect
Leave them young girls, to be tomorrow's healthy Mothers!
Perverts, allow them girls to realise their dreams.

They are conscious, their toxins compare to the venom of vipers,
Yet they cruelly disgorge that into the girls' pristine blood.
Contaminating and afflicting the young with doubled jeopardy.
Diabolically squeezing the vibrant life out of youthful hearts!
Uprooting blooming roses and casting them in the sun to wilt,
Mercilessly condemning the fledgling to a premature demise!

## Madhouse

Good morning,
Who is moaning?
This early in the morning,
Without a cause for mourning,
Moaning in the morning is mournful.
Stop these silly mourning moans and work.

Good afternoon Father,
You wish to pursue it further?
But it takes only birds of a feather,
To unite and fight their cause together,
Oneness can surmount insurmountable heights,
Gather around your family and select warriors to fight.

Ok warriors, rest tonight;
Night is a domain of the mighty,
Many were defeated in ill-waged fights,
Easy does it, patiently wait for the first light.
At the break of dawn deploy your faithful knights.
Where there is a will there is a way, don't despair soldier!

Wake up and be on the warfare soldier.
Be brave, strong and unmoved like a boulder,
Close the stable doors before the horse bolts away,
Eliminate despondency tearing apart our social fabric,
Restrain the bandits steering the reigns of the madding wagon.
Lest we are doomed and furthermore, continue mourning until night!

# Damn the gourd

I'm reeling in real confusion
Spare me the rasp my countrymen
I've enquired amongst my fellow plebs
They have all professed doubled ignorance
Since you're now up there, you might know better
What do you swear to, before drinking from the gourd?
Whatever it is, it is surely a good-for-nothing oath
It warps all the acuity in the right-minded
And they quickly forget their mandate
When they sip from the damn gourd
Instantaneously forgetting us!

Before the sip from the gourd,
We all mingled freely as comrades
We decided to send you to stand for us
Our plight was the armour you fought with
And you promised never to drink from the gourd
What is it that the damn gourd contains that is so potent?
Because only yesterday, in camaraderie union, we threw missiles
Rhyming, as we sang revolutionary songs against them
Protesting against their spendthrift and wickedness
But today, you're the first to condemn our vision
Vehemently denouncing us as a barbaric lot
I bet you were born different from us
But we shall all be there waiting

When you will dare come back,
With a mouthful of cheap propaganda
And try to explain that the sip was for our good
That we should send you back to represent us again
But alas, you shall meet the unprecedented rise of the plebeians.
And we shall tell you in your face that you hypocrite, go and hang!

## Speak no evil (12/09/2021)

If he is to confide in the reality,
You would be baffled in totality.
You may believe him, not a bit.
Yet that is the naked truth,
They lurk under long shadows.
All the same, he picks their silhouette.
They pretend they didn't say a word,
But his long ears hears,
That which distance drifts beyond.
For, even whispers echo.
And heartbeats can tell many tales.
He hears and sees their evil,
Yet he speaks NO evil!
He is civil and not a Devil.
He doesn't ride on people's flaws
But rather he derides gossip,
A perception of sheer perfection!

# The testament

Persons borne by the womb of a Woman,
Have enumerated days under the Sun,
But if death hunts me down at sunrise,
Those given days would all be forfeited.
What become of you my children?
Reject the embrace with inferiority,
Instead, sniff the sweet whiff of superiority
Because if death darken my door tonight,
What lay deep within me, would be vaulted.
Who will excavate the remains of my dreams?
Never falter near the manner I did,
Refuse to be divided along the maternal diversities.
Seek instead, the love and bond of paternal blood.
Blood is thicker than water; remember!
Only then, will you feel the throbs of my heartbeat.
If my name wakes up etched on Death's axe,
I shall depart from this Earth in haste,
Scurrying away from deeds adjudged the worst,
By the judgemental Saints' misplaced conceptions
And those who did not care listen to the sobs of my heart.
This is a Testament of Fatherly Love to you all I sired.
Love which some never got to know its feel and existence,
While others patiently waited for, until their hearts got tired.
Indeed, you can reject this testament as a hypocritical pastime.
You're all justified,
But if only you could walk my walk,
You would also proclaim the Testament!

## Mum witnesses (07/11/2021)

All the sparkling interiors of smoothened walls
Of these cosy, tall buildings caressing the skies
The linens which wrap sweating naked bodies
The unwavering, long and ghost-like curtains
Hanging down unconcerned, like weaned kittens
Unmoved by the demonic huffs and puffs of breath
The same with the gawking, indifferent roofs above
The rustling leaves of trees making thickets about
The cool breezes sweeping through forests abound
Together with the darkness of pitch-black nights
The sweet-scented, omniscient perfumes
They wear and spray in their posh cars and wrecks alike
All these things have ears and very big eyes
They see the wickedness of men – the naked evil prevailing
And hear the soulful moans of mourning victims
Followed by the resonant satanic purrs of the rapist
Yet, they all remain mum like mummified dead bodies
Oh Dear Elders, lend these crucial, but voiceless eye-witnesses
Even the faintest of voices you may find; we plead!
Lest our girl-child will continue to be molested
Under the watchful eyes of these witnesses' agonised gazes.

# Lies never lie

Beware of the ides of March!
The death knell rings,
But just not as much as it should,
Its eerie sound is rather encouraging than discouraging.
The pitfalls appear serene and flawless.

Some are handsome, athletic and charming.
While others are voluptuous and endearing,
The once lethargic laborious step is now agile.
The blemished scabby skin has been replenished.
Subtly reflecting a golden, caramel-like glow,
The skin's natural pigmentation wholly belied.

Red flags painted green to a red-herring.
By a verdant pigmentation which debars hearing.
Crimson warning signs subdued by a green dye.
Alas, shadowing all the danger warning signs.
Totally obfuscating the extant toxins,
But toxins cannot just be wished away, it's a lie.

But lies never lie forever,
They defiantly rise before the shaming gaze of world.
And another life is deceptively put on hold,
Yet a sermon behind a grave is just no sermon!
Why do we prefer living a lie to showing the spots?
And rather piteously die for believing green lies?

Dying while the death knell is sounding aloud,
To those with ears to hear the pleading wails.
And realise that, now is the time to abstain!
Proclaim safety; safety; safety,
Shun unprotected sex and be alive!
Run with your dear life, it is precious!
It cannot surely get wasted on the worst.
Beware of the ides of March!

## Believe

Beliefs are sacred; they are,
The ethereal mental apprehension of oneself,
The mental acceptance of our beings,
Those innate things that awaken our humanity
Because believing in oneself is by itself a virtue.

Everything else is but, hinged on what we believe.
Never doubt your worth and capabilities,
A grain of doubt sows disbelief in your abilities,
And debilitates your natural willpower.
Discover your beliefs and believe in them.

And they will manifest to attest who you are,
Believe, at least in what you cry for,
Bring every piece home to your heart and be at peace,
Believe to be alive and realise!

# When I'm drunk

I stagger and stumble as I wobble homewards
Heaving and panting between strides – at times backwards
My bulged eyes seeing nothing, but blurry figures ahead
Afraid of a number of ghostly silhouettes alive in my head
Seemingly accompanying me at a fearful distance
Hoping that I would sleepwalk and attack in an instant
I don't get fooled though; I remain alert and blink not a bit

If you snooze you lose but if you sneeze you get bitten
Pulling up a false stunt of invincibility, I put my Chibuku down
Onto a dark thing which looked like the head of a ghost
And *fearfully* sang on top of my lungs
Soothing, ageless songs of years gone by
And some songs I was taught by the Catechist!
The songs, most of which I remember
At situations like these – when I'm plastered and afraid!

When I'm drunk,
I talk ceaselessly and sometimes in tongues
Supplicating for my black sins, I commit behind scenes
And those left behind by my, of-long-gone ancestors.
Never forgetting sins by many others who do not partake,
Still, they call me a useless village drunkard

Yet pray for everyone and forgive too, ask my dog – Zulu,
It sins when it abandon me at late-night beer binges miles away
One of its grave sins was stealing my *chimunya*, years back.
I had left my sadza and *chimukuyu* on the hearth for the morrow,
Zulu and his cat friends ate it all and licked the plate clean.
While I was asleep, drunk!
I forgive him always, but only when I'm drunk!

## Strides of hope

Life is what you shape out when you still can.
Now is the time, procrastination is the thief of time.
Make determined strides towards life to claim it.

Be identified with the life your legs walked for.
Leave behind visible footprints of your strides of hope.
Hurdles and pitfalls waylay you, be bold and cope.

Remember fortune is rarely fortuitous but favours the brave,
Remember also that a fool's mind is as good as interred in a grave,
Exercise your mind, be clever and successfully chart your way up.

Determinedly maneuver around lest you flounder about.
You are destined to greatness, strive to live life abound.
A life aground is life without strides, a life without hope,

Strides of hope definitely carry the mind to its destination,
Scaling life's ladders to its hopeful summit,
Where dawn can be seen sun-raising a sunny life,
Take big strides of hope towards your hopes!

# Real nightmares

My bladder was painful but the road was crowded
The day was damn hot yet the sky was clouded
I didn't want it to rain, I was afraid I would get wet
The groin sensation I ignored, so I spoil not my date
I scanned around the area and saw kin eyes blinking
As if everyone knew about my little secret within

Perhaps my awkward step had betrayed me
Luckily, I saw a shrub at a curve up ahead
A perfect shield of the imminent vice in mind
I quickened my pace, but the bladder was unkind
The effort leaked something into my pipe
I hobbled on praying that the valves hold on tight

Before I got the shrub's complete shield
My zipper was down and some leaks dripping
I felt every muscle of my body loosening up
I groaned, but with relief as I drained away
All people who emerged from the blind side
Looked away in disgust as I messed their way

When I fumbled for my zipper once again
My eyes blinked open and there was no shrub
My zipper was up, but I was soaked wet and warm
'Oh, I am asleep and have actually wetted my bed!'
I realised, as the shameful morning routine beckoned
Those are the nightmares of reality in dreams

## My beloved is not mine

Like an eel, you slipped through my fingers.
Leaving me clung to painful tattered memories.
I wish you knew what is in me of devotion to you.
Only if wishes were horses,
I certainly would be riding into your heart always.
But I was overcame by a questioning heart beat
Of a confused questing heart.
Here I am now; on the other side of the love-divide line.

I was so blind to your undying love,
Real unadulterated feelings from your Heart
Just until you were gone – and gone forever!
It pains much to realise that, which I have lost.
I dearly miss that piece of me you went away with,
A piece I cannot really afford to commit to memory.
You were nothing to me once in my lifetime,
And I wasn't.
You are nothing to me now,
And you can never imagine of course,
How diverse these *nothings* are!

I think of you now,
When I can no longer have you,
More like sin in Death!
Where there was that piece which you took with you,
There is a dark, impenetrable scar now,
And it is painful memento of things gone by.
I know I can never have you back now,
But wherever you are,
And for whomever your heart feels,
Know that I still smell your sweet scent around me.
You are my beloved,
But my beloved is not mine!

**Let it be**

You can never tussle for love,
And still find it sweet!
You can never jostle for love,
And find it fascinating!
Deeds not words is a motto,
But never forget that:
Actions speak louder than words.
Relegation out of league,
Speaks for itself,
Even if you want resist it,
Desist from pestering for love.
New teams simply come on board.
And you find yourself in the cold.
In a conquest,
The victors conquer,
And the villains fall on waysides!
That is Love,
Let it be,
Every dog has its day,
Your day in love is on the way!

# A fairy-tale

The Sages say Patience is a virtue,
I was abound with it at childhood,
Yet often times, it left me in the woods.
Others say patience is bitter,
But its fruits are sweeter.
The imagination of sweet fruits tickled my senses.
And also spurred bubbles of coveted rarefied hopes,
That one day I would reap the sweetest Berries.

Hunched like a question mark,
I sat, every evening at our kitchen-hut stoep.
My unassuming gaze wandering about in a blank search,
Pausing when the silhouetted conical-shaped hue,
Stifled my stare to near concentration,
It was the roof of her mother's hut.
Ghostly jutting in the gloomy evening sky,
It could as well have been illusionary.

But I want to believe what I saw,
A shooting star shot before my gaze,
And poignantly fell over her mother's hut.
I ran back into the hut and snuggled near the fireplace.
That night I slept contentedly,
With her were awash my dreams.
And every night that followed,
As if she had suddenly metamorphosed onto my pillow.

Perhaps it was mere providence,
Otherworldly and whimsically providing,
For that which the heart and soul yearns,
Albeit, never in reality, but ethereally!
Still,
I did not lose heart.
In my dreams, we were wedded.

Yet I could not withstand her sight.

So much so that, if in reality,
Our meeting became inevitable,
I would tremble and scuttle in cowardice.
Or worse still, dive in the maize field and hide.
But every evening,
I wilfully searched the unfathomable grey skies.
For a vivid lustre of the shooting star,
To portend my destiny with my fairy-tale!

## Bundle of joy

The nine moons you spent ensconced in a dark world,
Alone, before gracing this world of light and darkness.
Moulded you into a master of trickery like a magician,
Causing her a grimace and a smile of pain and happiness
Yet you took it as a challenge and dealt with it headlong,
You wriggled, kicked, and punched to get attention.

Forcing the soft encasement to budge and bulge out.
Creating some space to zestfully wriggle and wiggle about.
She endured the pain and caressed her ballooned tummy,
Assuring you to hang on, the baking was still on-going,
Different ingredients would be added regularly.
One day it would be soil, which she always ate with gusto.

You would acknowledge and thank her with a deft punch,
Sending resounding echoes around the baking oven,
Causing mummy to squirm at quick spasms of pain and happiness,
The pain that you inflict while showing that you are bouncing,
Brings but joy to any mother, hence you are a bundle of joy.
Many a times you held her at ransom, yet you bring joy.

The atrocities you committed while in the oven.
You supplicate by generously displaying your toothless mouth.
Once in a while, you caused mummy to have stupid cravings,
One day you instigated for termites in July.
Where on earth could she get termites?
Yet she spent the whole day wallowing in July dust.

Despite of all the trouble you caused,
You are loved the most.
Welcome to the real world, mama's bundle of joy!
But remember, termites do bite!!!

## Mother's deathbed

My time on earth is now on flames
Snares of time have entangled my soul
Death is inevitable like the rise of the sun from the east
All these years, I have been battling with a chronic ailment
Like a rubber, its elasticity can stretch no more

I can cheat but, not death
Unless if I could borrow one of cat's nine lives
When I die, don't weep, wail or mourn
My spirit will always be around
Watching over you through your own eyes

When you miss conversing with me
Whisper to your Heart and you will hear my voice
When you need company to the village well
Take a nap and we will walk together in your dreams
Any day you wake up sad, go and stand before a mirror
Smile at the reflection that stares at you
I will smile back at you my child.

## Reasons …

Odd endearments build up in deep chambers of many hearts,
And erupt to the surface like volcanic molten magma.
Get unwrapped and laid bare for everyone to beckon.
Like gold, their authenticity is tested by fire.
To evaluate whether they are worthy reasons for love!

Some people believe fondness or passion,
Presupposes the true undying love,
Yet even fantasy does suffice.
Are there any reasonable enough reasons to love?
Reasons specifically meant to yield undying love?

Do reasons impact on the ultimate nature of love?
Love can be born out of awkward or even immoral reasons
While appealing and acceptable other reasons may seem,
Infatuation and fake love are born too.
Are there straitjacket logical reasons for love?

Reasons to love are as diverse as human perceptions.
Just like concrete mortar,
Other reasons concretise with time.
It simply takes the correct curing and proper tending.

Some mutual lifetime relationships spark at first sight.
Mere stumbling of soul mates upon one another,
Yet others denigrate it as a clueless and groundless start.
A preserve for the troubled souls, poised for doom.

# Don't you trust me?

A million dollar question that always works wonders.
But here I lay now, in a heap of bones wondering,
Couldn't I have withstood that devilish deception?
I now ask myself because I am beyond redemption.
My body is now destined for the ruins of a tomb.
Just because of that damned question!
Which I honestly answered dishonestly,
Instead of calling a spade by its name,
I cooingly answered in a near whisper,
'No I do.'
Though I subconsciously knew that it was a lie,
And my answer sounded my own death knell.

'Don't you trust me?'
You asked.
Yet you didn't even trust yourself.
You arrogated yourself the trust you hadn't earned,
And sapped dry the juicy of life out me.
If only I had been bold enough to say;
'Yes I don't!'
I'd have been still as healthy as a fiddle.
But here I lay languishing on this sore deathbed,
All because of a silly answer to a subtle question,
'Don't you trust me?!'

Naturally, it sounds so innocently appealing.
But it usually marks the demise of them girls.
Listen oh, to this infirm voice of another girl dying,
Actually dying for lying onto my heart where I got hurt
I lied because I respected a worthless man who laid me.
Afraid to hurt the feelings of a heartless ram,
Only the truth shall set you free girl child.

When this same question imploringly knocks on your door,

Be bold and answer for me and all those who died before me,
And say a thousand times and more, 'Yes I don't trust you,'
Oh yes don't barge, lest you'll end up a pile of bones like me,
Helplessly waiting to be unceremoniously bundled to my grave!
Where an epitaph that belie my true character will be erected,
Only if I was bold,
This day would surely have passed uneventful.
And I would still be mummy's vivacious little girl.

But very shortly,
I would be mummy's lasting painful memory.
A festering sore on her heart,
All because I couldn't simply say;
'Yes I don't!'
To the damned question;
'Don't you trust me?'

## Choices

More often, a golden urn frothing with poison,
Attracts dozens of eyes.
Completely ignoring a clay pot with honey,
What a folly if we can be easily swayed by looks!
Make your choice wisely son, lest you are doomed,
All that glitters is not gold, goes the old adage.

Even the Son of Man lamented and decried the naivety of men.
He beseeched and said, 'Beware of the Pharisees,'
They clean only the outside of the cup while inside it is filthy.
Woe to men who search for the purity of Pharisees in their looks.
Woe to men who judge a book by its cover, for they shall eat poison.

The lustre of a shining golden urn can be appealing,
While the dismal appearance of a clay pot is discouraging,
Yet it is that which lay within that should attract your heart.
Blessed are those men will who make good and careful choices,
For they shall enjoy the sweetness of honey in a clay pot,
Beware of this pitfall in choices, my Son!

Do not be easily smitten by mere glitters.
Beauty without character is ugliness.
But ugliness with character is beauty!
Seek therefore, the sanctity and purity of her heart, my Son.
It is often bestowed on clay pots than golden urns.
Shun the golden urns they are used to deceive only.

Apart from being poisonous, gold naturally invites thieves!
Remember the Sages say, they are those ugly caterpillars,
Which at the end of seasons, turn into beautiful butterflies,
So my Son,
A dirty clay pot with honey,
Is a far much better choice,
To a glittering golden urn full of poison!

## The myth of time

Inside the clock,
The cyclic never change,
Tick, tock, tick tock,
The hands of time move,
On the same path of time,
Yet outside the clock,
And at the same minute,
Of the same hour,
Yesterday,
Today,
And even tomorrow,
Something different stalks
The strokes of time
Still,
It is the same clock,
That attests to all events,
At whole different times,
It is the mystical myth of time!

## Centred chaos

Hopping like Kangaroos in the wilderness,
Stampeding like a confusion of Wildebeests,
A trending style of movement has seized the City!
Darting from side to side avoiding some random seats,
He saw it and abruptly stopped mid-hop,
To pay for one roasted mealie cob.
Roasted right at the heart of the Capital,

She halted too, a little late though,
She had already bumped onto him.
So did the young boy closely behind her heels.
Like a wave, they all bumbled into a sordid stinking corner.
A tomato and berry on sale were squashed in the process.
And all the vendors in vicinity swarmed the lad.
More like ancient Rome in the 8$^{th}$ Century.
Yet it is a modern-day City of 2018 AD.
But there is hullaballoo in the Capital!

Automobiles were painstakingly streaming,
Bonnet to tail in one lane snaking up,
While the other lane is jammed with fruit carts,
Engines belching, brakes screeching and horns honking,
Remonstrating to jay-walking pedestrians crossing,
As they compete with cars for space on the roads.
The pavements are seized with wild vending.
Do the City Fathers ever consider?
The plight of the disabled on wheelchairs!

A City that is a far-cry from a 21$^{st}$ Century Capital,
A haven for unruly and unimaginable tendencies!
At one intersection, automobiles have entangled into a doily.
As a Fun Cargo and another were racing against one way,
On the near side, a Hiace did not respect the rules of the road.
While a Caravan was maneuvering from the kerb,

Whereas a haulage was already turning left,
With a High-roof making a 3-point turn,
And everything else is history.
There is an unprecedented anarchy on the rise!

Man-made gullies, potholes and heaps of garbage all combine forces,
Making people and automobiles to invent a new maneuvering style,
Encroaching onto another's lane, bumping and scurrying is a norm,
Real fountains in the parks are clogged, antiquated and dry.
While irregular fountains erupt in the midst of roads on burst pipes,
Imagine car washing thriving in the City centre?

Intersections are gratuitously controlled by vagrants,
And the diabolic touting by the notorious *hwindis*,
Has been adopted as skill of trade by Money Changers,
The *dollar this! Dollar that,* shrills reverberates into an eerie cacophony,
Nauseating and menacingly polluting the once serene atmosphere.
With shoe vendors by right display their wares at *Bata's* pavement.
There is an unprecedented hullaballoo beyond restrain!
Oh Gracious God, help us restore our City,
To its olden Glory, the Sunshine City!

## Against odds (19/12/2022)

From another angle, they saw tears of happiness
Connoting an overreaching feat of limitlessness
On the other side they felt spheres of sadness
Wrapping a package stinking with limitedness

The contrast was comparably clear
The common thing was, only a tear
Yet the emotional drive totally vary
Because their weight of effort did not tally

The divide line was finally drawn
Creating a chasm between dusk and dawn
Akin to separating chaff from grain
Oops, the weaker went down the drain
As the dark clouds above threatened to rain!

The shrill of a whistle at the eleventh hour
Blew out a flame of hope flickering on the tower
Rekindling burning out embers, into a bonfire
Celebrating a victory won on a fired up arena
Sweet victory soaked with salted-sweat

Others saw it as a furious man's contorted smirk
While some saw it as a tired man's cheerful smile
Because, even a near miss is simply as good as a mile
File up comrades and receive your accolades
You have, against odds, conquered the World!

# Fantasies

A vast expanse of neatly manicured lawn,
Reflected against the sky with a hue of summer dawn,
As yellow, shrivelled leaves spiralled down,
Amusingly flaring about like a model clad in a gown,
A perceptible mellow fragrance of the Marula fruits,
Softly wafting in the humid summer airy into the sky,
The scenery was breath-taking, but he was lonely.
But out of nowhere, he got unusual company!
It was a girl, seemingly gliding on a white cloud,
Her white dress flaring against the azure sky,
Her face was dazzling with beauty,
She was gorgeous, an exquisite product of nature.
Yet she seemed wholly packaged for him,
He was mesmerised and simpered openly.
Beguiled by his charm, she smiled benignly.
A chemistry was triggered and flowed with emotions.
Overwhelmed by emotions, she mumbled something,
Her voice was soothing as a whisper of a summer breeze.
And as promising as a low hum of busy bees,
Altogether, meek sounding and sweet like a sugar stick.
He was hypnotised, fascinated and enlivened,
He outstretched his hands gesticulating a hug.
She flew her arms open as if bitten by a bug.
Akin to an angel flying from Heaven,
At a sweep of an impulse, they drifted closer and embraced.
Like two pieces of a puzzle falling into their place,
They gingerly and searchingly kissed!
Her effeminate lips dissolving on his masculine rubbery lips,
Stirring his loins almost to ecstasy,
He wanted to mumble a grumble,
But she put a finger on his lips.
He was surprised as much as confused.
A moment ago he was admiring nature,
But there he was in the hands of an Angel.

Godsend, who loved with her pure Heart!
Surprisingly choosing a sore festered soul,
A soul never been admired before.
Impulsively, their fingers entangled and she led him away.
Where was she taking him?
He desperately wondered in trance,
Perhaps to his grave,
He stiffened at that damning possibility.
He tried to wriggle and shake her loose,
Unfortunately, her grasp was firm!
Oh damn,
She is an Angel, not of love but of death!
Sent to shepherd him to his demise,
He realised, and trembled with great fear.
He pitifully pleaded with her for her love to dissolve.
But a pure heart doesn't easily undo its resolve.
Quavering and squirming, he woke up,
To a daring fantasy of dreams!
Ha Ha Ha!

# Birthday

Yellow and golden streaks on the eastern horizon,
Beckon the birth of just, but a different day.
Its new, tongue-like rays,
Licking the morning sky's gloomy haze away,
Wake up to a beautiful day and as the sun shines, make hay.
Never in your lifetime shall there be another day like today.

It is unique and its face has an emblem of happiness,
A befitting souvenir of your journey in life,
It is another stride of a worthwhile journey.
Looking back over your shoulder,
You shall see, as you grow older,
The imprints of your footprints,
As testimony that you, like others,
Have had also, your unbridled chance,
And journeyed alongside world's greatest men,
The smiling face of this rare day is a good omen,
Harbingering good things which lie in days beyond,

On this day, years back,
A seed sown some months earlier germinated.
Cherish the day today for its fruits,
It is a day more defining than other days.
A day that marks a notable shift in your life,
What a folly, many a people falter,
On this ought-to-be great, yet fateful day!
Keep your guard up, do not over-indulge.
Lest you shall stumble and miss the mark,
It ought to be a special day in all respects,
But alas, it can easily be your Doomsday!
The very day when dearest dreams collapse,
For God's sake, it is your birthday,
Many things can wait for another day,
But just not the occasion heralded by this day!

Having valiantly resisted the demonic forces,
You cannot be vilified on one of your few special days.

The day is reckoned just once and never again!
Today is a day of unparalleled character,
A day that defines who you're,
Cherish the day and endear its memories,
Hold it special and revere it with esteem.
Enjoy it fully, thus to make it count,
Happy birthday!

## Builders

builders, of course,
but not the trowel;
the spirit level;
some bricks;
even the mortar;
oh, he is just being reminded,
there is NOT even the space to build upon!

# Faithful servants

The clutch of the talons of hunger was painful,
On the malnourished flesh of faithful servants.
With each day that lapsed the pain became unbearable,
And triggered an unprecedented exodus of masses,
Robbing the nation of its populace and workforce alike,
Which braved the thorny paths and croc infested rivers,
To cross the borders, shaking off the fangs of poverty,
Rather preferring the devil they didn't know properly.
The grass home wilted while it was green across the river,
It required sheer determination to get to the green-lands.

Lest we not forget however, the unwavering spirit comrades.
Of all those who remained resolute aboard a sinking ship,
Indefatigably watering the withered grass with tears and sweat,
Amidst the relentless waves of chaotic hopelessness and quits
Where a runaway hyperinflation diabolically seized the economy,
When bus fares could increase innumerable times,
Whilst one is actually busy flagging down lifts at a bus stop.
When prices could triple while one is fumbling about a wallet,
Making the amount in the wallet a mere fraction of the fare,
Yet these people faithfully reported at their workplaces daily.
When that which they were paid in the name of a salary,
Could miraculously shrink beyond value in sheer seconds!
Yet they unquestioningly continued in service of their Country.
In a pitiful environment where basic commodities were scarce,
With food as scarce as hen's teeth, but they remained resolute!

These Comrades steadfastly toiled and soldiered-on at sunrise,
Despite wallowing in dire poverty and the dust of dusk at sunset,
When only sheer hope and determination carried the day!
Many died, hoping that tomorrow would be a better day,
But to their despair, *tomorrow* was an uglier replica of yesterday.
More than a decade now, and nothing has been said about them.

The faithful people; true heroes and heroines – real comrades!

Selfless comrades who sacrificed not only their lives, but,
The lives of those many others who depended on them,
Comrades who valiantly fought to keep the sinking ship buoyant,
Comrades who weathered the storm of marauding hunger.
These are the near forgotten comrades,
The unsung Heroes and Heroines of yesteryears, today and
tomorrow!
A workforce which endured the calamities of years 2007 and 2008,
But never surrendered, never voiced quits.
A heart yearns to see these heroes and heroines remembered.
Just a little consideration!

## He left his things

It was never easy turning his back to leave
He got to resist the urge of going back and live
Better, his mind insists that he goes far away
Leave everything; carry nothing on his way

His heart is bleeding, seemingly to his sure death
If he dies, he got to be buried somewhere on earth
Reach out to those who were there when he was born
Ask them where they buried his birth-right before he is gone
He ought to lick the soil to initiate his rebirth

It's never easy for a stranger to be readily welcomed
Suspicious looks and strange language is the norm
But even a strangest stranger ought to have a home
He now lives with new folks away from his kith and kin
His heart is healing as he plays with new cats and kittens

A toad will only be seen in daytime when it is in danger
The sword of Damocles hung precariously over his head
He left his things and left – went where the path led him
Where a home away from home ushered him to settle
Fired up, he lit a fire under a Marula tree and put a kettle

Where the morning sun emerges behind a beautiful mountain
Its colourful rays spreading over the morning sky like fountains
Giant baobab trees majestically standing like dutiful Sentinels
To which the sun nod subtle salute before drowning, always

# Behind the stables

There is an oasis of calmness on their tables,
And a façade of a rancid stench behind the stables,
These stinking corners behind the beyond,
Call out our names when we are homebound,
You will hear the echoes of our responses
The soiled crumbs from their tables,
We scavenge and make our coveted meal,
Yet when they visit us with their friends,
They feed us good.
Their friends are thrilled,
And commend them for their care.
They unashamedly accept these undue compliments,

Let me tell you, friends of my Masters,
It is a mere picturesque façade
Professionally painted on the walls behind the Stables,
We're suffering at the hands of our Masters.
Yet we're ordered to be cheerful as if we are before our Pastors.
To augment the façade of mastery of their Lordship,
Listen to the inner voice, you friends of my Masters.
We're not living in bliss behind the Stables!
We are now fed up of living a lie.

Burst sewage pipes are fixed only when their visit is imminent,
Vendors, Beggars and Vagrants are bundled up.
That is when the danger posed by potholes and debris is realised.
They feel vulnerable and patch up the roads and collect refuse,
While we, the Plebeians are regarded the indomitable lot!
They give us what they regard as safe drinking water,
Which they dare not even bath their dogs,
They tell you we have competent health delivery services,
Yet they are swiftly airlifted to hospitals we cannot even pronounce,
They proclaim excellent standards of Education.

But their children are in your countries tapping on real good
Education.

Friends of my Masters, listen to this inner voice.
Peer through the smokescreen and see what's hidden beyond.
Away from your sight, behind their tables,
There lie the dilapidated stinking Stables,
Our home!
All what you're made to see,
Is the picturesque façade that belie reality!
We're here behind the Stables,
Supplicating and waiting for a Moses to be led to Canaan.
Our Masters are enjoying the honey and milk,
But never really want to share.
They tell us to bring our own cows and bees,
If we are to enjoy the honey and milk with them!

## Kinsmen

Has water now gained dominion over blood?
'Blood is thicker than water,'
I thought I knew what it meant.
Only until yesterday!
When kinship disintegrated before our eyes
Kinship can now be washed off like stains.
Perhaps the contemporary soaps are mighty.
Why is hatred seeped into the hearts of our children?
Aren't we supposed to be all under that tree?
That majestic fig tree,
All gathered and carefree.
Sharing constructive ideas and cherishing,
Good fortunes coming the way of the kindred.
But you my brethren,
Endure severe heartaches,
At the manifestation of success upon a kin,
What is it that evokes your happiness my kinsmen?
Is it the downfall and indigence of a brother?
Does the demise of kindred inspire joy in you?

When brethren take strides towards success,
You cast prickles, hurdles and pitfalls on the path.
And when a kin is pricked, bumbled and stumbled,
Jeers, ululations, and drum beats are sounded.
Isn't a wife married by a kin, a wife for the clan?
A pickaxe acquired by a kin, an excavation tool,
To clear the stumps in the whole clan's fields,
Rejoice when a kin prospers, for it is for us all.
Do not dilute kinship blood, it loses viscosity!
And then water thickens, hatred supplanting Love.
You, me, them, us, we're a kinship! Let's not hate.

## Let it rain

Please, let it rain,
Let it rain and dissolve the mounds and moulds of pain,
The pain we are reaping in our fields instead of grain.
Let the raindrops cowardly hit our parched, starved faces,
And erode away the wrinkles of hopelessness.
Always permanently knit on our brows,
As we sadly peer at the gloomy skies of many days.
While rainy clouds are drifting to the western horizon,
Being shepherded by a crowd of empty, dark clouds,
Stained with propaganda, oppression and poverty
Please, our summer rainy-clouds drift from the west
Cause a westerly breeze to blow back the rainy clouds
And it will rain on the land of our forefathers,
In the same manner it does far and wide.
Perhaps some bold droplets may puddle,
Into small pools and drown our sorrows.
Maybe misery and despair may flow downstream,
Together with the brainwash awash the ideology of goons,
Please, let it rain!

## God

Allow me Brethren, let me ask.
In whose presence is my God?
Or should I rephrase and ask again,
In which congregation is our God?
Help me, oh dear Prophet,
The anointed man of God,
Confusion is turning my head topsy-turvy.
Once, the path was certain and without pattern,
Behind the long shrouding curtains it now is uncertain
Why many shredded paths to the Kingdom of God?
When all what we seek is Salvation!
At dawn, clergymen appear to have a common cause,
Praying and praising the Lord our God!
But like herd men, they gather their sheep at dusk.
And build new kraals for the same old flock
From which God are they departing?
And to which God man of cloth?
Are you in service to a new God now?
What of the God in the former congregation?
Help me understand, dear men of God!
Why the diversity Brethren?
Why specifically your ministry Pastor?
Overnight, man of God has become a man of Gold!
While your congregants wallow in dire poverty?
And you fervently preach their Years of turnaround!
Yet it's you they turn around and prosper?
You don't tolerate questioning, I know.
It is how demons manifest in your eyes,
But as humane as you are,
You know that half of the world knows your deceit.
But you castigate them as those of little faith.
Heathens who need anointing from the Anointed!

## Two idiots

One told the other,
The other told one,
Yet the one being told was not there,
While the other was,
When they told one another,
All the same,
Either one or the other,
Told another,
Unless,
Both the one and the other,
Talked not to one another,
But the one listened to the other.
Saying nought,
And the other talked not about it,
Perhaps,
Both had just nothing in offing.
Yet they keep on pointing filthy fingers at each other,
Hoping that we get fooled and forget their idiocy!

## Letter to my brother

I didn't want to bother you,
But its because I have failed to fit,
Those shoes are still oversized brother.

Did you know, Brother?
My chin is full-bearded now.
My feet have also grown to full size,

But alas, I still cannot fit in your shoes.
Yet the task you assigned me is long overdue,
And nobody is willing to relieve me of the burden.

Thorns and prickles have bored pores on my feet,
I have no choice, for I do not have shoes.
But I have to embark on this journey.

My heart yearns to fit in the shoes you left,
So that I can take up where you left,
And pursue your living dreams to the end of time.

Until then, I trudge, hobble and, wobble barefooted,
To realise the dream that you held dear at heart.
Not a dream of fallacies, but a dream of passion.
A dream of ink-full pens drooling at the agony of the World!

# Handmade love

Can people love because they made love?
Or they make love because they love?
Does making love invariably make people love?
And make them compatible and inseparable.

Does making love make marriages?
Perhaps, it is love that makes marriages.
Can people really make lasting love without making love?
Help me out of Wonderland!

Someone furtively whispered into my ear,
People make love when they're married!
But I know them two, who got married,
Well after they had made love.

Wasn't it making love which married them?
Isn't it brothers and sisters, handmade love?
Upon a man-made marriage,
Can handmade love sustain a marriage?

Do man-made marriages suppress love?
And wither the plant of marriage.
Does making love really make repelling hearts attract?
Or it is because of the sown seed, that love is sewn together!

## Sullen heart

When the ice-cold look drilled into his eyes,
A spasm of pain tore his heart apart,
Like an early summer lightning bolt.

When his eyes met that cold tepid look,
Fiery tears rolled down his cheeks,
Eroding all his self-esteem and pride,

Dissolving and wasting his dignity.
Drenching his mind into a painful fathom,
Reminiscing of the good old days!

When her eyes gleamed with pure devotion
And her touch tickled his sensual feelings.
When her heartbeat was akin to a love song.

Caressing his heart to sleep like a lullaby
When her heartbeat was pure sweet rhythm,
And could really entrance his heart,

Alas and alack, it's all water under the bridge.
The melodies and whispers have since ebbed out.
Fading into the distant horizon like a setting sun!

## Rhetoric mantras

Deep guttural voices reverberate in our ears.
Subconsciously evoking in us, sadness and tears
While acclamations and ululations echo in squalls
Against the precipices of the distant mountains
While stupefied monkeys and baboons look on
Hanging precariously on flimsy twigs wondering
What has induced happiness in mankind below?
Aren't these bellows usual rhetoric mantras?

As if the concerns of the primates got me enlightened,
I began to wonder while to a knot, my heart tightened,
Haven't I heard these silly talks once, but countless times?
I learnt in third grade that empty vessels make the loudest noise.
Our revered school motto even went, 'deeds not words',
I was promised yesterday, promised today and,
I will definitely be promised again tomorrow.
Should I remain content, floating on fake promises?

What is the motive of parroting mantras?
Is it to keep men on tenterhooks?
Perhaps to confuse women,
After failing to convince us?
Should we stand by and be taken for a ride?
Who should hold them accountable?
So that we may see the break of dawn,
Before we break down,
Let's get rid of these rhetoric mantras,
The fallaciousness in them all is too insulting!

## Dear Daughter (28/07/2021)

Hello,
Dear Daughter, hello!
Listen to your Father's advice.
A boy he was once, remember!
Take no pride in frolics with boys,
Boys will take you on a ride,
For a damn ride without a right,
So please, have a clear conscience.

Define your own principles,
Flow not with the trending waves.
Lest they could be treading their heels,
Beyond the distant hills to doomsday!
Never glide with, 'the tide'.
Its sheer weakness!
Say no to peer pressure.
Shun their ways and shine like a star.

Show your character like a fish,
Swim upstream against odds,
When they, like boulders, and all,
Unquestioningly roll downstream.
In a doomed youthful bandwagon,
Not you, Dear Daughter, No.
Set yourself apart!

## Silhouetted reflections

A blurry recollection of the days of Yesteryear still lingers.
Days when eating chicken gizzards made children forget their kin.
When the authenticity of meat was merely a butcher's bluish streak,
Then, rice and chicken was as covetous a meal as is pizza now.
When the ripple effects of Christmas days were so intense,
When one could truly long the taste of bread and butter,
A time when the majority citizenry was naturally patriotic,
Days when patriotism was natural and not partisanly defined,
When allegiances were wholeheartedly pledged for national cause,
And the national anthem and colours, inspired pride in every citizen.
When modesty, decorum and respect was our untainted heritage,
When we were everybody's keeper, your child, my child!
An era when seasons of the year were never changing,
Days when sheer skin pigment elevated some to superiority,
When the inferior class was relegated to subjects of the superior,
And minnows revolted against the Masters to defeat these ideologies.
It's funny, how these ideologies have gradually gravitated back at us.
Subjugation blatantly propagated by a brother on another brother!
Forcing reflections of the past to flicker in our fading memories,
Like moonlit silhouetted tree shadows on a late summer night.
Reality making it painful and unbearable than reflections,
The irony of reflecting ugly face of the bittersweet past!
While looking at the skewed face of the present
A bittersweet agony of our fore-fathers,
Glean the good out of the dim past,
And strive to make today good
For a better tomorrow!

## Motherly

Despite being a two year old baby
You show deep motherly instincts
You are a crawling baby,
Yet you yearn for babies.
You know a baby needs care!
And a baby needs love.
You cry and wail to be strapped,
Yet you cuddle and strap dolls.
You cannot bath your body,
But you know a doll needs a bath
Your mother sings for you
And you sing to a doll too
A baby to your understanding,
A baby heart in you!
Showing pure motherly devotion,
It all spews from the motherly heart
All what I see in you a little princess!
When you are playing on your own,
A motherly heart in the making!

## Dear Stranger

I have trudged around dreary furrows of earth,
Hobbled across deserted deserts and valleys,
Peered into cracks and crevices of distant caves,
Hunting for the shadow of a rare Stranger,
Perhaps my existence can be so justified.
Come back stranger and dazzle my mind,
With the lustre of your white, starry eyes,
That radiated a silver glow onto my heart,
Instantly thawing a frozen indifferent heart
Sensitising an endearing ambiance to a lone soul,
It is the impression of that expressionless look,
That secretly narrated a thousand untold stories,
It is that homely but true smile,
That captured and imprisoned my soul.
A mere stranger, unknown to any emotion,
Yet you evoked known feelings.
Feelings that overflowed and demonised my spirit,
When courage to hold a steady gaze deserted me,
I glanced sideways and blinked countless times
When I thought I could look straight into your eyes
Alas, and like dew under the rays of a morning sun,
You had melted into thin air – gone!
Leaving my heart precariously hung in its cavity.
With a Stranger's image embedded deep within,
Oh why dear Stranger, why?
Why did you disappear just a minute earlier?

## Gloomy night (20/03/2020)

Darkness quickly replaced evening dusk.
Dismally plunging the earth into a dreary haze
Dampening the sparkle of a beautiful day,
Happiness swallowed by the gloomy expanse of the sky

And strangely, a shredded moon mournfully hung.
Like an abandoned ornamental gourd,
Appearing like one giant tear-brimmed eye,
Piteously staring down the earth wondering.

Why panic, pandemic, pandemonium and fear,
Has suddenly gripped this wonderful land below,
Startling humanity beyond comprehension,
Forsaking their routines, hobbies and habits,

Every soul dashing for the nearest bolthole
Like roaches scampering for unfumigated cracks on the wall.
Such was the ordeal of humanity on one sombre night!
When the rumble and roar of the sky shook the earth

# Distant shadows

silhouetted distant shadows
waltz before his cold strained eyes
causing odd reflections on ice
of horses, beggars and wishes too.

if only he were the grubby walls
which the shadows are gleefully licking
he wouldn't be wishing or imagining
but experiencing the feel of their tongues

they attract furtive peeps of strangers,
and keen puzzled peers
of perplexed passers-by,
cherishing the beauty of distant shadows

his fingertips itch to softly caress
sketching out the shadowy outline
nonchalantly nodding back and forth,
to a wheeze of his curious breath's puff

they appear golden like summer sunset shades
beautiful like a rainbow reflection,
across the slanting, sunlit rain showers
behold, the beauty of distant shadows

## Brave faces

Never ever envy us,
As we mill around the streets
Wearing brazen brave faces
Daring and taunting death itself
And you wish you were like us
With a never-say-die attitude,
As if we have a choice?
We are a miserable folk
Either we hustle or we starve.
The conundrum of the masses
A deadly virus on the streets
And smiting hunger indoors
That is the fate of a poor man,
Whose affordable self-isolation,
Is nothing else but a drainpipe!
Hence the brave faces
Masking fear and helplessness
Stirring deep within us
Every second longer
That we linger on the streets,
Timidly dodging and staving,
The powerful fangs of Death,
Remember us Oh Lord!

## Hands of time

In our unfortunate circumstances
I hate to be that person in your life
Whom you remember with a contorted face
The very person who causes an adrenaline rush
The damn companion of Sorrow
Who robbed your happiness and left a hollow
It was neither by design nor my desire
I despise the person I turned out to be
A personality which belies my real wish
And all that which is attributed to my being
I can never take away now
And how it pains me too
But alas
The pain of pain is never made less
Because another person professes pain
Although deep inside myself
My Soul is at pains
These past demeanors
Like unexorcised demons of yesteryear
Haunts me whenever I stroll down memory lane
Reflecting back and forth in my mind
And like a ghost at a feast
My past tend to almost always resurface
Irritating like that tiny mosquito
That simply doesn't gets tired of singing
Even to an already besieged ear
And in all earnest, I'm sorry
To be the fiery sword
Painfully lodged in your heart
I regret to be the source of your pain
Only if I could turn the hands of time
I would make sure
I am the very person you remember
With a cheerful longing smile on your face

## Dawn

A tired haze benignly glare in the sky
Down the eastern horizon imbued in a greyish hue
A tint proclaiming the lapse of the ultimatum,
Night begrudgingly folds its blanket of darkness,
The duel between light and darkness is over
Darkness throws in the towel and bows out
It cannot linger any longer, light has conquered
Unimaginably stifling the serenity of Earth
Albeit, darkness will live to another day
Tonight!

# When...

When diverse perceptions cease to define political divides
When conflicting ideologies are no longer used to draw battle lines
When those with different views are no longer persecuted
When all political haranguing is for the goodness of the society
When freedom of speech does not forfeit freedom after speech
When the revered August House demonstrate its augustness
When cruel whips crack no more on the backs of the electorate
When they are of the people, by the people and for the people
When treachery and coercion cease to wage their ugly faces to the
masses
When fundamental rights are not given by the right and withdrawn
by the left
When shackles and manacles are for murderers and not opponents
When the eyes of the Law see equality in all who come before it
When manipulation of the plebiscite has taken to the hills, scurrying
When they are ashamed to peddle cheap propaganda and skewed
ideologies
When mantras and mantras after mantras are a thing of the past
When respect for the Citizenry reign supreme
When they truly frown at oligarchy and an epitaph for Corruption
stands to its demise
When the rivers of Honey and Milk flow again, and anyhow
Without being cunningly propagated into their backyards
Only then, shall I become a proud national
And bear true allegiance to my Country
And sing the national anthem by heart and my soul
And bow to the flag wherever I see it,
Even when it's flying at the prison gate that I am about to be jailed
It would then be flying in honor of my State
And earned its respect!

## The folly of a man

He stood there long and his mind stood by.
Amused by a distant speck of mirage,
Frenziedly shimmering on the horizon.
He stood as if he wished he was the forest.
He stood there long as if he had an inkling,
He would lie there forever in forlorn,
And ruffled by his ghostly presence,
A snake slithered into its hole.
Waiting for the loner to dare get at it.
He did not know he was siting a grave.
On a land where no grave ever sat.
Yet a grave of a lone soldier was beckoning,
In a manner the horizon beckons at the sun,
On a gloomy winter sunset.
If he had spared a moment of thought,
No grave would have stood there.
But of his own hand and at his own time,
He tirelessly dug,
Inching deep into the Earth,
Until a mournful yawning pit gawked,
Where the fool together with his tools of trade,
Were both unceremoniously buried,
In a grave of their own making,
At a gravesite of own choice,
When people pass by this tomb,
They hardly guess correctly.
'There lies another idiot who, by his hand interred self',
In a dusty shelf of a lone grave!

## Little flower

Oh, little flower!
Bloom and brighten,
Our dull-looking days,
Moonless nights with dim stars,
Rain-dripping days with no sun-rays,
Overcast skies with clouds dark like scars.
Bloom over sullen hearts of souls wandering on earth,
All those searching for brighter days before their death
As your miniscule petals opens, oh, little flower.
Tear apart our sorrow pursed lips also,
Albeit, for the faintest smile possible,
And the Earth would be a better place.

## The hideout

Oh, my Oh!
Fat wallet
Cheerful smiles flash
Seductive looks shine up
Sweet music blares about
Cached cash vapours
Cold beer floods around
Drowning a poor man along
Into sorrows of the morrow
When the wallet frowns empty
Wiped damn clean in a trance
At a Hideout in the hiding!

## Imaginations

I vividly recall myself when I was a carefree first grader
Unashamedly responding to the popular 'when I grow up' question
With all sorts of funny, constantly vacillating fancy wannabe's
But I turned out to be a poet, cutting across them all dreams

If the realisation, why I didn't become a pilot begins to haunt
I fly my pen on paper and its ink like the fumes, also leaves a sign
Artfully taxiing it between the parallel lines of the writing pad
The black ink, like skid marks, streaks indelible marks on paper
If why I didn't become a guitarist comes knocking like a beggar
I send it packing by artfully streaming up idle synonyms of guitar

When I was young, I also dreamt of being a President
Yes! A people's president and the most favourite of all!
But here I am now, an adult in a completely different world
A skewed world, more of an underworld to the noble minded
Where the dreams I held closely to my bosom as a youngster
Remain mere cloistered virtues my heart eternally holds

Indefinitely condemned to remain haunting hallucinations
Converted into painful reflections and imaginations of my past
Turning my life into a hollow manifestation of eerie emptiness
But like their children, I also imagined and dreamt of a future
Little did I know that my life would be a reflection of torture!
A reflection of dreams and imaginations of a spun pendulum!

# Hope

Despair and hopelessness,
Fatigue and dejection,
Have all ganged up against Hope.
Shepherding hope to stinking peripheries,
Where hope coagulates even in daytime,
Into sheer hopelessness,
Yet –,
Yet all that which spurs humanity is hope!
Hope that tomorrow would turn out a better day.
Forever better and even best,
Hope that tomorrow *shall* never die.
Alas,
Not in this lifetime.
The future has never been so bleak,
Confrontation with desperation is now a norm.
Men's daily bread!
Yet it's written, 'men cannot live on bread alone.'
Day in, day out,
Every second that ticks,
Hope is gradually ebbing away,
Drifting farther into the marshlands,
Where no hope can be salvaged,
In a miserable livelihood of depleted hope,
With Peoples who simply hope against hope.
Labouring under clogged veins of hope!
Killing life before the lapse of its lifetime!

## Gone to the dogs

It really is something.
But just not anything,
That it really ought to be.
Not even anything,
That anyone ever imagined.
Not at all something,
That they wanted.
Yet there it is,
Something that has lost its symbolism,
A renegade to the spirit of Ubuntu,
Like salt that has lost its saltiness.
Yes, it is still there
But it has eventually gone to the dogs!

## My wish

If you were a fruit my daughter,
I would wish you were an apple,
Which,
As faithful as the sun,
Remains attached,
Onto the scabby and shabby branches
Of the very tree that bore it,
Despite it turning mellow and juicy
As it ripens with time,
Religiously hanging,
Even when its fall becomes inevitable as death,
Still,
An apple does not fall far from the tree!

# Future

Today is just too grumpy for near comfort.
Like an angry and cruel chubby step-mother.
Today, isn't smiling!
It is harsh, moody and edgy,
Today is, and More!
Sure, I can hear moos from cows,
The lows signal milking time,
Even the aroma of fresh milk,
Is discernible as it pervades the air around,
Fusing with their expensive cologne,
And the vile stench,
Of my fermented sweat,
And tears of penury,
Induced by the relentless licks of the long fiery tongue,
Of the unashamedly naked sun on my scabby skin,
As I toil all day long,
Yet I sleep on a drained stomach.
While they swim in perennial rivers,
Of the nourishing milk,
And the soothing sweet honey.

## Sweet memories

Take me to that mountain at the bus stop
I want to climb to mountain top
To consult an elderly *Sangoma*
Who has seen it all!
Because almost always
Sweet memories linger longer
And like stubborn stains
They live to fade another day
But not memories of yesteryears
And as if Yesteryear was yesterday
Old memories licked my chapped lips
They quavered with a sweetened shy
Evoking the treasured vaulted memories
Of once upon a time along a highway
A highway tarred with Love and happiness
When love simply meant, 'us'
Lovebirds that were made out of love
Even in strangest places and;
Out of funny things under the sun
Places like long stretching highways
Things like mere yesteryear songs
Chocking and drowning sweet memories
Deep down the unfathomable depths
Of two happy Hearts
All the while, lovingly waltzing
To a rare serenade of *kwela-kwela*

**Wishes**

He stands at the river bank thinking
Squinting at the dazzle of the sunrise
Wondering why she is always drifting

Downstream, afloat a turbulent flow
Every morning; every sunrise; every day
Farther away to the shores of his heart

No flow of a river can be touched twice.
Yet he keeps on longing to touch her
Perhaps his fingers might tickle her again

He let his troubled mind float on his wish
A dazzling speck appeared downstream
He imagined on one of the days of his life

The tide rippling with her out of his heart
Would miraculously reverse and flow upstream
Providently drifting back into his heart

## Silent whispers

More often than not,
Hearts begin as strangers yesterday,
They stumble on each other today.
And converse in silent whispers,
In a language foreign,
Even to the wits of the witty.
They sing serenades in unison.
Dancing to the percussions,
Of a strange rhythm of their heartbeats,
Until the tepid sun nods for sunset,
And the scintillating bells of dusk sounds.
But –,
But when the jingles of dawn awake them,
With a startled start tomorrow,
They find their voices and screamed;
*We are strangers no more!*

# My beloved (to the once Sunshine City)

With squinted eyes, you stared at the glare of a cheerful sunrise,
As you woke up, bubbling with happiness and pure satisfaction.
And plunged into a warm and rejuvenating pool of Sunshine,
Thirsty tongues of the sun's rays licked your glowing face.
The sunshine shone and illuminated your beautiful smile.

Your companionship was longed by folks and strangers alike.
Everything about you was just perfect like a new prefect
Then came along sunset, suddenly stealing the glow away,
The sun, like a fireball slowly smouldered the entire horizon.
Forcefully drowning you in a cold pool of darkness.

The twinkling stars never appeared,
The moon was dull and hazy like a rusting silver penny.
What gnawed at your beauty my Beloved?
Your vivaciousness all gone overnight, what happened?
Who mutilated your face, who besmirched your character?

You woke up to the same cheerful sunrise as you always did,
But today you are downcast and shy, soiled real badly.
You stink to high heaven, like a drunkard in a drunken stupor.
Sweat, tears, saliva, pee, shit and blood putrefying your body.
Leaving the once-beautiful and lovely body a sure gangrene!

## Love

Love is true,
It honestly tells its own tale.
Love is translucent,
One can easily see through it.
Love is sensational,
It evokes deep sentiments.
Love is phenomenal,
One can tell when it is in the air,
Like a morning breeze,
Softly caressing even leaves,
While slapping at faces of loners.
Love is reciprocal,
It loves what loves it.
Love is certain,
It is unquestioning to its love.
Yet Love is jealous,
It simply turns green at times.
Love is a wonderful feeling,
It naturally flows into a Heart.
Love is perceptible,
It can never really, be disguised.
And like a long forgotten seed,
On fertile soils of low-lying vleis,
Love can sprout when least expected.
Love doesn't grow old,
It has no age!
Most importantly, love doesn't fade,
It renews itself naturally.
Love is extremely mystical,
It can be found by many,
But is understood by a few.
Love, can find its Love.

# Tears

Let me cry,
Let tears swell up in my eyes.
Let them bulge and sag on my eyelids,
Never wipe them off,
They are not crocodile tears,
Neither are they tears of shame nor fear.
Let them freely and slowly roll down my cheeks.
As rivulets of the lasting testimonies of my desires,
They simply are the tell tales of deep-seated emotions.
Feelings which must not be suppressed,
Because they may never get understood,
Let the warmth of tears thaw my benumbed eyes,
Perhaps my cold look will go away forever.

## Grandfather's letter

Dear Future,
Today is harsh and cruel!
I peek and peer into you,
Through the creaking crevices,
Cracking on the weather-bitten door,
That is keeping you at bay,
Beyond reach of a poor man's shrivelled arm,
I have resigned myself to a peeping-tom
Anxiously gazing and wondering,
What do you hold in store for me?
I search for the slightest of signs,
The faintest of the tell-tales,
Of what's riding on the clouds.
But I see only, a shimmering mirage.
A smouldering, smoky and sooty future!
Yet my hope against hope is on you.
For a dawn to a long night ending,
Shirking the gloomy of darkness,
Bedevilling both today and yesterday,
My arms yearn to embrace,
The goodness of a new day with a shiny sun,
The serenity of a dusk with bright twinkling stars,
A semblance of a better day, a better tomorrow,
Hear my plight, oh dear good Future.
Lest my grandchildren also be condemned,
To the same damning fate,
At the hands of Today!

# The blindfold (18/09/2021)

Take up your Swords and Daggers
Search the dim alleys and isles before dark
Peer even, in the crevices of dreary caves,
Don't forget the mausoleums of the long dead.
Spare not, the expansive mansions and expensive palaces,
Hunt for the shameless daring rapist.
Who deflowered our Lady Justice defiling her sacredness?
And soiling her wholesomeness

Go out there in numbers and sniff out,
The thief that stole the blindfold of Lady Justice,
Exposing her to the immorality of humanity,
The evil winks of wicked men's eyes.
Tilting the scales of justice blushing,
Succumbing to the irresistible charm of the elite,
Yet, the filthiness of the poor man,
Nauseate her to look away.
Her once sharp, double-edged sword,
Is now a fist-blunt gavel!
Punishing <u>Only</u>, the persecuted poor man!
For she now administers justice, but <u>Not</u> blindly!
Disaster is looming comrades, disaster!

Lady Justice has clearly abandoned her call.
Weights on her scales have little significance.
When the worse comes to the worst,
She adds weights to a side of her choice.
She now reads the Law to her liking.
Brethrens, lady Justice is no longer blind,
Her sanctity has been blown by the wind,
Only when justice is seen to be done on her rapist,
Would Lady Justice restore her true character and being.
As an honourable lady who is not spiteful, corruptible, partial or
partisan!

# Footfalls of the night

Eerie sounds on the dead of the night
Thudding heavily onto the sad ground
Lumbered and laboured
Like those of a thousand, tired labourers
Filtering through the thickness of darkness
Into subconscious ears of haunted souls
Disturbing the serenity of the night
Whose footfalls are they?
They can never be from any mortal being
But –
It can only be Witches and Wizards
On their routine nocturnal patrols
Alas, but you have been heard, better luck in hell

## Youthful madness (07/11/2021)

Gripped under the vice-grip of a murderous vice,
The fledgling have all run amok,
A ferocious wave is sweeping the youths
Into the dungeons of madness,
Ravaging the society like a wild inferno
Madness madder than real madness!
Madness which sicken the brain
Let us not be judgmental.
A frog does not scale the fence if the ground is cool,
Why are the youths getting wasted with waste?
Doing the unimaginable?
Like anesthetised zombies,
Could it be idleness?
For an idle mind, is the Devil's workshop!
The youths,
In whose hands our future lies,
Are lying through-out the day,
Blacked-out to consciousness,
What will become of my society?
If a stitch in time really saves nine,
Let us stand up as a society
And nip in the bud this vice of youthful madness
To avoid a bleak future,
Rise and clamour, No to Drugs
We might salvage,
Just, but something from the debris of the future!

## Understand

When the tell-tales sounds, trumpet in your ears,
Hear them; play deaf at your own peril!
When the harbingering omens suddenly appear,
Clear as early stars in the evening sky,
Grasp the meaning, don't act dumb.
Love is no Game of Thrones
It is never won in battlefields,
No hero has been honoured for battle of love.
Never grapple for it therefore!

Love by nature, isn't violent.
Love grows in lovely fields,
Where, loving men are the farmers,
And women lovingly tend to the plants until harvest.
When Love gives you its back, never dare go for its tail,
Love has teeth; it can even bite your fingers,
And still go,
Leaving you doubled up, with a bleeding heart,
Together with painful wounds!

Just let be and let it go!
The moment the die is cast, the deed is done!
Unfortunately, the choice was made and it was not you.
You can never tussle for love, and still find it sweet!
You can never jostle for it, and find it fascinating!
Deeds not words, is a motto, but just don't forget:
Actions speak louder than words.
Relegation out of an elite league speaks for itself,
Even when you may want to resist,

Desist from scrambling for Love
You will be dumped but with scars of love,
No matter how battle-hardened you are,
Smart suitors would be deemed suitable,

And you find yourself under the table
Love is not conquest, but a beautiful show
The exhibitor with a heart whispering, woos the bride,
Not the 'I will not go down without a fight' losers,
Love is humble, love is considerate,
Love understands, please understand!

## Cowards

We chant slogans renouncing them
But you don *apolo*-jerseys at dawn
We sing for a Revolution in unison
You sell us out to the men in uniform
Dining with the enemy, boot licking
Swinging ludicrous scoffs at us
Mercenaries who snitch on our cause
We are booted and bludgeoned to death
The curse of innocent blood will dog you
To the graves of your great grandchildren

## Tree of wisdom

Sadly
The big old tree has fallen
Our soothing shade is gone
The searing sun will fry us alive
Some not-so-strong westerly winds will shake us
While the squally wintry winds sting our faces
The big old tree has fallen
It has gone to the ruins
However
We celebrate its life
The life it gave to the hopeless
The legacy of wisdom it pollinated
All these years it majestically and steadfastly stood
Swaying back and forth
At the hands of relentless hailstorms
But, it couldn't cheat age
Eventually, it gave up the fight
Its stump will forever live
In life and memory
We will long those moments
We spent under the shade of the old, big tree
Alas, it will never be there again!

## Long question

He has, but only,
A blurred memory of her mum,
His heart has, but somewhat a,
Lonesome memory of his childhood
His mind is, but rather a,
Very blank cavity devoid of love
Where is mother's love?
Who can quench his  quest?
Answering his long question!

When others brag,
About her unmatched, her unfailing love,
He, knows not what to say to his peers!
He does not remember her smile.
She never hugged him, never pampered him.
She simply left him to grow,
On his own like an indigenous tree!
The roots of which knows no tending,
What is a mother to this man?

# Herd boy's prayer

I wish the moon of my hopes could rise and shine
To sparkle in my life like a jewel in clean water
While the stars of my dreams twinkle
Shepherding home a brighter tomorrow

I wish the sun of my happiness may rise,
And thaw away my sad feelings
May the river of my satisfaction overflow
And flood my forlorn heart

I wish the clouds in me never overcast
They will shadow and dampen my spirit
May my rain gently fall and never pour
Lest it pokes pores on my thick skin

I wish my sky be azure and translucent
So that I never experience dark days ever
May the wind in me never blow in whirls
Preserving my footprints of hope in the paddocks

Please, may the anger of abuse never froth
And I remain as calm as an abandoned glass
So that I remain in control of my senses
Driving all my cattle to the pen
Like a happy herd boy!

## Betrayal

Alone, I blundered
It was witnessed by none
A word I never said
No soul heard anything
Nobody knew about it
Therefore, I worry not
Safe is the little secret;
Yet I know no peace since,
Piecing up silly excuses!
To justify my deed,
And explain my silence,
My conscience is at war always,
The price of betrayal.

# Die another day

The time gong,
'Tick-tock; tick-tock',
Are thuds of ticking time
Inside a diligent clock of life,
Alerting the incurious bystanders,
Of the impending hunt around the clock,
By the damn hands of time, in time!
Still, minutes of life ticked away.
But in a blink of an eye,
Time was chocked,
And it stopped!

In no time,
There was no time.
But a shrinking lifetime,
The twilight stars popped up,
While the sentries of life dosed off.
And the gloomy evening sky sulked,
Yet at the demise of time, the demons awoke!
And walked naked at the dead of time hunting,
For those daring, Godforsaken goons,
To choke and snap their bones,
But the hunt went awry and;
A lifetime got revived,
With just but a,
Snap of bones!

## Before we wedded

Hello there, answer me please.
What your mother told you, I wonder.
I always think about you when I feel sleepy.
Perhaps my mind would be tired,
From all-day long attempts,
To banish you from my thoughts ever,
I hear your yells, "Daddy, Daddy, hear me!"
As you also search deep within your fragile heart,

In vain I try to figure out the name,
Your mother deemed befitting for you.
A name floating on both her happiness and sorrow,
On the one hand, shooing me out of her mind,
While on the other, keeping me adrift around her,
Hello there, answer me please.
I am your Father, your very biological father.
It was complicated, you'll never understand.

We met at the crossroads with your mother.
However, I shouldn't have said nothing,
I queried and waved goodbye at your mother.
Weaving my way, as far away from her as I could,
I was afraid she could catch up with me.
And heave her bulging belly at my face again.
I scuttled for dear life.
As if she was a monster!

When I was content I was alone,
I sighed, relieved and forgot what I sired
I also forgot all about what had happened behind,
That is how we divorced before we wedded!
I deviously subtracted myself
From their family before I even got added
Hello there, answer me please,
Where are you?

# Curiosity

The waiting,
Imaginations,
Anticipation,
All glared
Like hungry toddlers
After the plain porridge meal
Is deliberately delayed
By an ugly, cruel stepmother
To late mid-morning
When the monster hunger
Has sapped all happiness
And sadness has stirred curious thoughts.
Curiosity always heighten the tension

## A Lamentation and half

I was pure; I was a virgin!
No finger of a man had felt my body.
All men venerated me.
I was the cradle of self-esteem for my society.
Then along came a wolf in sheep's skin,
And defiled my sanctity with the callousness of a devil,
Took away my treasure and never looked back.
Never bothered to patch up the wounds and bruises,
It was mission accomplished, no need for damage control.
You saw no reason for social responsibility.
As long as my priceless jewel was, but sparkling in your hand.
You robbed me and my kinsmen!

You left us all empty-handed.
I was their only hope out of Egypt to Canaan.
I was, but their sacred oasis in a desert.
I was, but the pristine plains of *Chiyadzwa* diamond fields.
I was, but *Mucheka wakasungabeta,* the mountain-range of gold.
I was but, their everything,
Yet today;
I am, but the worst whore ever, who betrayed their trust.
I am, but the dumpsite which reeks with stinking fetid of immorality,
I am, but the 'Pool of Death' at Epworth – a threat to humanity.
I am, but the painful reminder of their robbed treasures.
A lasting memory of exploited resources!

# Woman of woes

Is it morning glory?
Far from it!
She endures a morning gory
With woes and moans,
Of a woman wearing,
And tearing with abuse!
In dreary mourning gowns,
While others put on,
Dearly morning gowns!

Her peers wrap,
Smooth, cotton bathing towels,
Yet she braves,
Bashing shovels and gavels!
Gritting her teeth in pain,
Is her morning greeting.
More like eating gravel.
She has a dirty label

A woman of woes,
When their tears wells,
With joy and happiness,
She tears in fear,
Sorrow, sadness and misery
Tears which tear,
Her heart to shreds,
Despair beyond repair!

## White granules

The youths knew but kept it in laughter
No elder right-guessed that it was disaster
Neither the wisest, nor the intellects
Until the ugly phenomenon came naked

It was all blank, paused gazes everywhere
Nobody stirred since it appeared harmless
'Some useless white granules,' thought the elders
'Beware of mistaking it for coarse salt'

Warned an elderly man with a white crown for hair
'But it is tasteless; it's useless in the kitchen'
Retorted one woman who had touched it
On that, everyone began to move away

Silent were the youth, as if they knew nothing
Yet they were waiting for the elders to disperse
They scrambled for the useless white granules
They ingested the granules inhaling smoke

The granules suddenly send them off balance
Engulfing them with the uselessness
Meant by the women answering the elderly man
The society is suddenly robbed of its youth
By the useless salt-like, tasteless grains

# The path

There is light at the end of the path
This long, winding path with rocky patches
Trek on it  towards your life's horizon
Where all rise on the pedestal of Dreams

The hue of dawn beckons like a beacon
Colourful like the pulpit of a Deacon
Behind the colour, lies your life's worthy
Tear down the shawl of dawn to be wealthy

Early birds catch the fattest worm
Wake up and bath in dew before it gets warm
Before the worms of life burrow into the ground
No worm risks to be picked at noon

Rise on your dreams and follow your path
Nobody will walk your walk, do your part
Never wish you were in another person's path
Paths are different, be the author of your destiny

The horizon is your destination
Time of arrival revolves around your estimation
But procrastination is the thief of time!

## Songs and cries

The crooning heartbeat hums,
Thudding sentiments of impediments
Groaning at the cruel blows of thugs
Bleating the long-since suppressed truths
Buzzing the dull echoes of silent tales
From the graves of unsung heroes
Tombs with epitaphs which read, 'plutos'

The painful thud of the heart perseveres
Purring all mournful songs of the decade
To those who shed innocent blood and forget
Bleeping tones of a suppressed citizenry
Where what is good is dictated by the goons
Beeps of professionals drowning in abject poverty
While non-professionals swim in milky honey

The heavy heartbeat of sorrow palpitate
Reverberating the muffled cries of sadness
Stagnant in deepest crevices of the poor's heart
Chocking poor souls of desperate masses
Penned in the kraal of destitution and starvation
The heartbeat echoes soulful songs of hope and;
Thuds the mournful cries for Salvation

# The debt

The intensity of my breath waned
The chest movements slackened
My veins and arteries weakened

The clarity of my voice diminished
Slowly, my mind got benumbed
Causing my faculties to go astray

The throb of my heart ebbed away
Still, I heard the timekeeper's gong
It's peculiar, eerie shrill made me realise

That death was lurking in odd, dark clouds,
I was due to set off towards west, to the waste
To square up the inescapable debt with my creator,

So, one of these day I shall wake up dazed
All senses, like startled birds, flown away
Both my eyes wide open but with no gaze

Clouded with a blank, otherworldly stare
Dazzled by a glary flash of an ethereal flare
Sight on eyeballs forever frozen dead

I will set off alone, on a very long journey
Let the Baobab be the symbol of my departure
Its soothing shade is good for the long journey ahead

## Advice

Don't get too fascinated
Because you might get fastened
Onto the hinges of things which belong in the past
It could be the attitudes that keep you wallowing in the dust
Or the very mind-set which made you an outcast
Linger, not longer; lest you be dragged along
And left stuck, trapped in marshy lands of a past era
Sing not anymore, sombre tunes of sadness
Bring not along, the shadows of sad memories
They often turn out as distracting memoirs
Don't be held at ransom by flaws of the past
Pay attention, never lose sight though
Of all past activities, they are good for hindsight
Glean the important lessons for tomorrow

Stare at your shadowed moments
No longer than it matters
Because, just a glance sooner than later
May in the nick of time
Fortuitously provide a fairer glimpse
Of that which you have been searching
Remember, when one door closes
Another door often opens
Be wise not to miss the door ajar
While waiting for the closed door to open again
Some doors can only be opened from the outside
And it takes solely the right person
Which, unfortunately might not be you!

## The angry sun

When the sun rise angry
It shall sulkily spread its fiery rays
Which appear like giant silver fingers
Meant to roast alive all creatures out of line
Its mouth will be like a furnace of hell
Breathing fire roasting the earth
Waging a sizzling hot war
Burning all scumbags

When the sun gets angry
It shoots its hot tongue down
To lick the earth clean of immorality
And like spears, pierce to death the tainted
And those cruel stonehearted leaders
Who thrive on oppressive laws
Beware of the Sun's rage

When the sun flames up
It frowns and dims its brightness
Hunt for nude mind-sets in darkness
Those who thrive on mortal unchaste nakedness
Shepherding them into the wilderness
To torch down their wickedness
With flames of anger!

# Take a step back

Blood knows nothing.
Neither race, gender, colour,
Nor hate, love or friendship,
It doesn't change colour for any,
It remains red, ready to flow.
The moment when the flow flaws,
It spells danger, usually death follows.
To humanity and fauna alike,
Show me he who has black blood?
Causing bad blood amongst us!

## Mind swing

Sometimes I cry
Over things I try and fail
Unfortunately, failure leaves a trail
Like scars and tattoos, it is symbolised
Shamefully, I try to hide my sad face away
From the piercing, derisive eyes of triumphant failure

Sometimes I smile
Over things I try and succeed
Golden ideas I went for while miles away
Galloping on white horses to mark a milestone of success
With many more smiles on faces of the loved ones, kith and kin
I enjoy the last laugh with failure licking its fresh wounds, defeated!

# Tears of Africa

From time immemorial, she has been weeping,
Bleeding from the wounds of years preceding
And even years on the horizon, beckoning
Wounds without dark scars for they never heal
Wounds which the stars of Africa never illuminate
Perfunctorily sutured wounds to deceive Africa
They shamelessly ride on silly make-believe stunts
Yet the wounds reek with fetid pus and maggots
Eating away mother Africa's flesh to the bone
Her fifty-three children all sit around her at dusk
Their hungry eyes blinded by excavator's fine dust
The fireplace is cold, yet another cold evening story
Yet another empty night and still, no one is sorry
All her children depend upon mother Africa's fending
And to provide, she has to be up and about, standing
But she is weak, her blood has been mercilessly sapped
Her precious milk is gluttonously sucked by bullies
Her energy is indifferently disgorged from her; wasted!
Mother Africa is now frail, with a sickly body
Her breast milk has been laced with a slow poison
To gradually kill her suckling children
Her wells and rivers are rapidly drying up
Deforestation is stripping her to near nakedness
Clouds of black fumes float, polluting her skies
Holes and tunnels are snares and pitfalls to her children
Degradation is eating her away shrinking her in size
In the end, tears of helplessness roll down her cheeks

# His Grace

I swam in flooding, crocodile infested rivers
Climbed quite a number of sacred mountains,
Defiantly defiled the sanctity of many caves
Boisterously rode on the back of Devil's horses
Dined with the Devil like a denizen of cloud nine

The crocodiles feasted on the salty flesh of many
Some friends got swallowed by mists in the mountains,
Others lost their way out of the caves we ventured
Whereas scores more rode into oblivion on runaway horses
Meanwhile, quite a number crashed aloft cloud nine

Amongst them were Saints who still weep in their graves
The hungry crocodiles crawled onto their doorsteps
The bolting Devil's horses simply dragged them along
When the thick mist in the mountains just blinded their eyes
As cloud nine got overwhelmed and caved-in on them

Now, if it wasn't for God's pitiful eyes
You have taken quite a good guess;
I would definitely be a hazy memory to many
A faint shadow of the long-dead ghosts
Glory be to the Lord, our God

The eyes of mercy spotted me in wilderness
And God saved me from drowning in wickedness
His Grace is upon my poor soul
I shall forever glorify his mighty name, Amen!

## Faithful Companion (31 October 2022 Car Crash)

Goodbye Fielder
Goodbye my companion
For a lasting number of years
You were my faithful companion
We blended as if joined in communion
A friend in need, you were a friend indeed
So loyal you were, my wish was your command
We traversed the vast expanse of plains and mountains
When the silhouette of death encroached onto my way
Its stinking odour heavily pervading the evening air
You stepped up and blocked a jab aimed at me
Bravely burying death under your shadow
Averting a sad walk to my demise
And the smelly mouth of death
Was forcibly shut, empty
 By a martyrish crash

## Angeline

More like an archangel
Superintending hordes of earth-angels
Through an angelical symbiotic semblance
Your angelic face glows like embers
Dazzling many who dare stare gaping
As your starry-white eyes gaze back
Punctuated by a seamless meek smile
Drilling small dimples on your cheeks
Smouldering many hearts of men
Sending even, short tongues wagging
Drooling at your beautiful, slender body
Mesmerized by the angelic beauty
Of a willowy Angel

## Pain of love

There is, but one painful pain; the pain of love
The type that has hands, it can hold you close
Pain that has a heart, it can choose who to hurt
Pain that is blessed with eyes to watch you suffer
I fear most, pain that has a mouth, it taunts
The worst is pain that has legs, it can follow you

With love, great pain is in putting up with dead memories
When love, like a ghost becomes a lasting memory
A breathing memento of the sweetest ever told stories
A reminiscence of the old huts where hearts lived in happiness
Yet, it is now all in the history books of two lives
The kind of pain that chooses who to hate and hurt

Pain which invites you to peer in the not-so-distance past
Prompting a gush of hot tears to boil down your cheeks
Seeing the once gleeful smile turn into a derisive smirk
Benumbed by the cold stare of the same warmth-radiating eyes
Hearing the sad whispers of the once love melting voice
Being awakened by the irritating nudge of taunting pain

Watching as the flames of love flicker and waltz goodbye
As the very person who used to evoke good memories
Slowly becomes a faint memory of vivid love
When love walks along with you, but at arm's length
A constant reminder that you cannot touch the same water twice
The pain of loving and living, if love was a creature!

## Voice of Wisdom

Echoes of a resolute old voice reverberate
Rumbling from the depth of underground crevices
Like a grumble of a tired, waning thunderstorm
Receding into the armpits of sullen mountains
Resounding a familiar caress to our forlorn hearts
With a faint taint of determined, but tired crackling
Last felt years back when family time was prime
Granny would sit us under a majestic old tree at dusk
When the dust of laborious afternoon activities settle
And tell us folktales of old good friends – mortar and pestle
Legendary tales of how lion was king of the jungle
Intriguing tales of hare almost always outwitting baboon
Sacred mountains, forests, caves, and animals
Learning the rich traditions which upholds Ubuntu
Under the soothing foliage of the sacred, huge tree
With granny leaning her back onto its trunk
As if to tap some wisdom off the old gigantic tree
I listen to granny's voice now, the same way I did back then
And easily find wisdom in her old tales
The same way I didn't find reason in her resolute
I visit the sacred tree now, often scared to find granny there
The same fear I felt when I imagined finding granny not there
Under the gigantic old tree of wisdom, ready to impart wisdom
At dusk; when all afternoon dust is settling like roosting birds

# The dock

Confrontation with conscience,
Actuates moral blameworthiness.
And guilty conscience stir up remorsefulness,
From the unfathomable depths of the inner being.
Radiating a pardon plea,
In the eyes of the guilty conscious.
But what happens in the psyche of the innocent ?
When the gallery and the Judge alike are oblivious,
That before them is a sacrificial scapegoat,
Never near guilty!

Rumbling and grumbling
At any attempts of innocent protestations.
He sprays his innocent eyes across the courtroom,
It is dark!
A sombre atmosphere is gradually descending,
Threatening to crush and grind
Any traces of innocence.
Pounding a guilty powder souvenir,
That shall outlive innocence!

But Why, My Lord Why?
What is Guilty as Charged?
Why sacrifice those not guilty?
Why are the Not Guilty baptised Guilty?
Making them as guilty as a cat in a goldfish bowel?
When they are as innocent as an unborn child.
Fascinating it is, to a bystander.
Mindboggling it is, to the Pure.
The not guilty, pronounced guilty is painful,
Belittling and inhumane!

## Learned friends

Follow your souls' desire,
Let your hearts not tire,
Boldly scale up the legal tiers,
Soar and glide on clouds of certainty,
In the skies of the elite fraternity,
Among a flock of learned colleagues.
Exercise your legal minds on legality.
Let also your legal eyes see equality,
Litigating professionally and ethically,
As you opine differently on legal principles
Defending and standing for justice.
Your dream, your sole desire!

## Gone

when yesteryear memories
like mighty perennial rivers
turbulently flood our minds
exposing many marooned hopes
and invigorating faded dreams
of a tomorrow we all wish for
adorned with blissful dreams
cut out not from the old cloth
of the forgotten beautiful past
then, yesterday mirrors tomorrow
and tomorrow dies before sunrise
to be mourned in the afternoon dust
before we plunge into evening dusk
like tired, migrating ducks
still, tomorrow will be gone!

# Over my shoulder

Have you ever been poor?
So poor that you breathe sparingly,
Afraid that, like every poor man's mealie meal,
Oxygen might unexpectedly deplete.
I mean so poor,
That you shorten your strides when you walk,
Afraid that they may quickly take you to doomsday.
Poverty which makes you reluctant to open your door,
For fear of being slapped by a gust of poor, cold wind.
Damn poor that you hate your even shadow,
Believing it's the curse that's always with you.
Very poor that you always wake up with bloodshot eyes,
Because you mourn your poorness in your sleep.
Well, I have been,
That is why I cherish every morsel I get!

## What does death do?

We know, they are alone lying
The same way they were lonely, dying
While their children were promising to come, lying
Until their souls wheezed out flying
And their bodies turned stiff retiring
Tired of holding onto life after a long clinging
By their death,  we ask wondering and sighing
Did death conquer or it was defeated during their trying times?
They died many years before death came along
What does death do to dead people alive?
Them killed by neglect than death itself
Forgotten alive by the fruits of their wombs
Yet they lie still under the weight of earth mounds
Which are their lone graves scattered in the woods
Again abandoned, and forever in death
What does death do to dead people in graves?
Does it take them back to us?
To find us our old selves – unconcerned!

# A psalm of love

Take me back to where I belong
The day you read this, know its been long
Alone, I have tried in vain to get along
Eventually, I have realised that I'm forlorn
Take me back to where I came from

Allow me a glimpse of the good old days
When your eyes shone on me like morning sunrays
And your touch felt like cool drops of summer rains
Its all gone, as if it were one bad dream of no gain
Let me back into your heart where I suffer no pain

Look back and flash your electrocuting smile
Be agile for any eventuality because it's been a while
Let's walk hand in hand around the village for miles
That way the moon and the stars will shine on us
Celebrating a rarefied reunion of soulmates

Lead me to the bottommost of your love
Sow me and lovingly wait for love to sprout
And glamorously soar in the sky like a dove
Flying up not with jealous or spite, but Love.
Take me back my beloved!

Take back my love and lay it on your pillow
Caress it gently and watch it attractively billow
Shaping up beautifully like branches of a Willow
Then bloom below your face like a stylo plant
Take me back my darling
And forever breathe the fragrance of love

**Mmap New African Poets Series**

If you have enjoyed *Strides of Hope*, consider these other fine books in the **New African Poets Series** from *Mwanaka Media and Publishing*:

*I Threw a Star in a Wine Glass* by Fethi Sassi
*Best New African Poets 2017 Anthology* by Tendai R Mwanaka and Daniel Da Purificacao
*Logbook Written by a Drifter* by Tendai Rinos Mwanaka
*Mad Bob Republic: Bloodlines, Bile and a Crying Child* by Tendai Rinos Mwanaka
*Zimbolicious Poetry Vol 1* by Tendai R Mwanaka and Edward Dzonze
*Zimbolicious Poetry Vol 2* by Tendai R Mwanaka and Edward Dzonze
*Zimbolicious: An Anthology of Zimbabwean Literature and Arts, Vol 3* by Tendai Mwanaka
*Under The Steel Yoke* by Jabulani Mzinyathi
*Fly in a Beehive* by Thato Tshukudu
*Bounding for Light* by Richard Mbuthia
*Sentiments* by Jackson Matimba
*Best New African Poets 2018 Anthology* by Tendai R Mwanaka and Nsah Mala
*Words That Matter* by Gerry Sikazwe
*The Ungendered* by Delia Watterson
*Ghetto Symphony* by Mandla Mavolwane
*Sky for a Foreign Bird* by Fethi Sassi
*A Portrait of Defiance* by Tendai Rinos Mwanaka
*Zimbolicious: An Anthology of Zimbabwean Literature and Arts, Vol 4* by Tendai Mwanaka and Jabulani Mzinyathi
*When Escape Becomes the only Lover* by Tendai R Mwanaka
ويس مَرُ للَّيَلُ فَى ثِفتَي...وَلَاعَمَام by Fethi Sassi
*A Letter to the President* by Mbizo Chirasha
*This is not a poem* by Richard Inya
*Pressed flowers* by John Eppel
*Righteous Indignation* by Jabulani Mzinyathi:

*Blooming Cactus* by Mikateko Mbambo
*Rhythm of Life* by Olivia Ngozi Osouha
*Travellers Gather Dust and Lust* by Gabriel Awuah Mainoo
*Chitungwiza Mushamukuru: An Anthology from Zimbabwe's Biggest Ghetto Town* by Tendai Rinos Mwanaka
*Zimbolicious: An Anthology of Zimbabwean Literature and Arts, Vol 5* by Tendai Mwanaka
*Because Sadness is Beautiful?* by Tanaka Chidora
*Of Fresh Bloom and Smoke* by Abigail George
*Shades of Black* by Edward Dzonze
*Best New African Poets 2020 Anthology* by Tendai Rinos Mwanaka, Lorna Telma Zita and Balddine Moussa
*This Body is an Empty Vessel* by Beaton Galafa
*Between Places* by Tendai Rinos Mwanaka
*Best New African Poets 2021 Anthology* by Tendai Rinos Mwanaka, Lorna Telma Zita and Balddine Moussa
*Zimbolicious: An Anthology of Zimbabwean Literature and Arts, Vol 6* by Tendai Mwanaka and Chenjerai Mhondera
*A Matter of Inclusion* by Chad Norman
*Keeping the Sun Secret* by Mariel Awendit
مكتوبتكلّ سجلّه by Tendai Rinos Mwanaka
*Ghetto Blues* by Tendai Rinos Mwanaka
*Zimbolicious: An Anthology of Zimbabwean Literature and Arts, Vol 7* by Tendai Rinos Mwanaka and Tanaka Chidora
*Best New African Poets 2022 Anthology* by Tendai Rinos Mwanaka and Helder Simbad
*Dark Lines of History* by Sithembele Isaac Xhegwana

**Soon to be released**

*a sky is falling* by Nica Cornell
*The politics of Life* by Mandhla Mavolwane
*Death of a Statue* by Samuel Chuma
*Along the way* by Jabulani Mzinyathi

https://facebook.com/MwanakaMediaAndPublishing/

Printed in the United States
by Baker & Taylor Publisher Services